FIGHTING SHIPS

WORLD WAR 11
AIRCRAFT CARRIER

Richard Humble

Franklin Watts
London · New York · Toronto · Sydney

© Franklin Watts 1988

First published in Great Britain in
1988 by
Franklin Watts
12A Golden Square
London W1

First published in the USA by
Franklin Watts Inc.
387 Park Avenue South
New York
N.Y.10016

First published in Australia by
Franklin Watts Australia
14 Mars Road
Lane Cove
NSW 2066

UK edition ISBN: 0 86313 742 3
US edition ISBN: 0-531-10639-X
Library of Congress Catalog Card
No: 88-50375

Designer: Ben White
Picture research: Jan Croot
Illustrations: Pete Chesterton,
Doug Harker, Kevin Lyles

Map: Hayward Art Group

Photographs: Imperial War
Museum, US Navy Photographs

Printed in Belgium

Contents

The flattop at war

The years 1941–5 saw the greatest sea battles of World War II, fought in the Pacific Ocean between the fleets of the United States and Japan. Because of the coming of air power, these battles were fought with the help of a new weapon in naval warfare: the aircraft carrier, or flattop, as American sailors called it.

Flying aircraft off ships was first seen as an ideal way of scouting for enemy ships at long range. But when aircraft became capable of carrying bombs and torpedoes, the aircraft carrier became a weapon. Its aircraft could attack enemy ships at distances far beyond the range of the heaviest battleship guns of the day, without the two fleets ever sighting each other.

Before the coming of the aircraft carrier, the fighting sailor's job was to get his ship within the range where its guns and torpedoes could damage the enemy most.

▷ Aboard the carrier
Lexington crewmen
inspect SBD Dauntless
aircraft which have
returned to the ship after
a strike mission in March
1942.

4

Carrier sailors, on the other hand, had to launch and recover aircraft; fuel, rearm, and repair them between flights; and man the guns to beat off enemy aircraft.

Life aboard these floating airfields was always dangerous. Unlike battleships, aircraft carriers were not protected from enemy attack by armor plate. They had to carry explosive aviation fuel known as AVGAS to keep the aircraft flying. And to cope with the vast distances of the Pacific Ocean, the American and Japanese carrier fleets often had to stay at sea for weeks at a time, supported far from base by fast fuel tankers and supply ships.

◁ On the busy flight deck of an American carrier, aircraft are recovered after a mission. An Avenger torpedo-bomber, damaged in battle and trailing smoke, is about to touch down on deck. Other planes line up for landing.

A floating city

The aircraft carrier was the biggest, most complicated war machine ever devised. It was a floating city, and, like all cities, its different areas had different functions.

The bridge, from which the carrier was navigated and commanded, was perched high in the "island" on the starboard side of the flight deck, which ran from bow to stern. The engine room housed the engines which drove not only the ship, but also the generators which supplied every corner of it with electric power. The seamen kept the ship clean and in constant working order; trained mechanics serviced the aircraft; special crews handled the aircraft on deck. But every man on board had the same ultimate job: to enable the ship to launch and recover aircraft.

△ How the United States Navy supplied its carrier fleet at sea. Here the fuel tanker *Merrimack* refuels an aircraft carrier on one side and a destroyer on the other. The date is July 1945 and the American fleet, after fighting its way across the Pacific, is preparing to attack Japan.

▽ Broadside view of an Essex-class fleet carrier: 250 m (820 ft) long at the waterline, capable of steaming at 33 knots, able to carry up to 100 aircraft, with a complement or crew strength of 3,500 men.

Island

Elevator

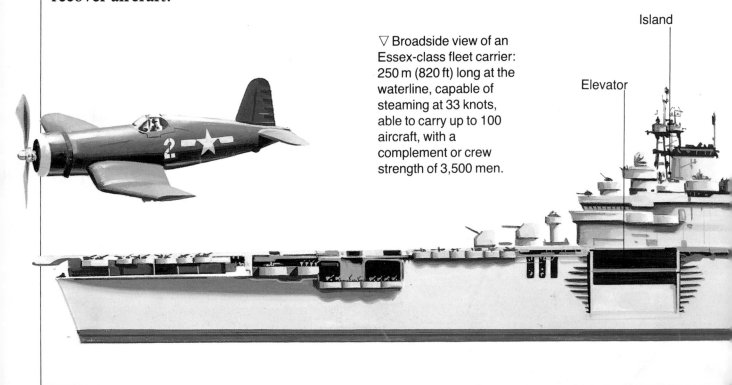

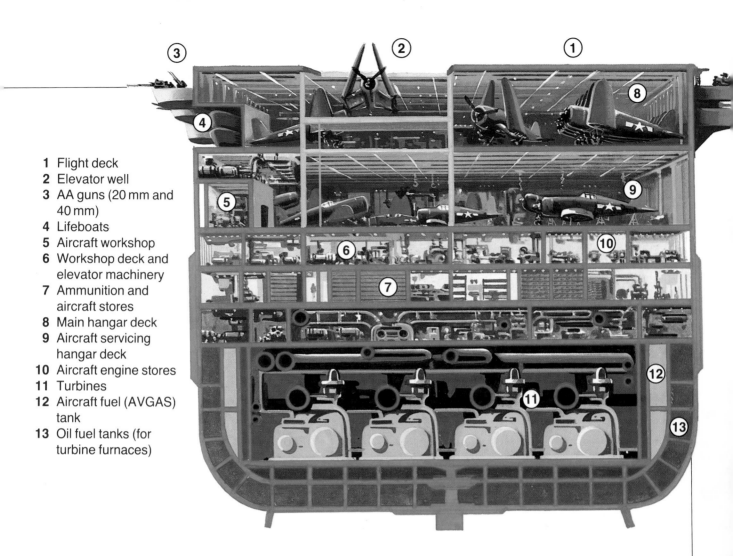

1 Flight deck
2 Elevator well
3 AA guns (20 mm and 40 mm)
4 Lifeboats
5 Aircraft workshop
6 Workshop deck and elevator machinery
7 Ammunition and aircraft stores
8 Main hangar deck
9 Aircraft servicing hangar deck
10 Aircraft engine stores
11 Turbines
12 Aircraft fuel (AVGAS) tank
13 Oil fuel tanks (for turbine furnaces)

△ Cutaway view through an Essex-class carrier, the mainstay of the American carrier fleet. The ship's massive engines were geared turbines, able to deliver 150,000 horsepower to the four propellers.

Flight deck

Below the planking of the flight deck, the carrier's uppermost layer, lay a descending maze of working and living areas. Heavy elevators delivered aircraft to and from the hangar decks below. Further down were the mess decks and bunk areas where the men ate and slept. The giant engines and fuel tanks were located below the waterline.

Life on board

American sailors in World War II, especially those on big ships like aircraft carriers, were luckier than those of most other navies. The US Navy led the world in providing the best possible equipment and facilities for its crews.

The sailors' clothing – from dress uniforms for shore leave duty to working overalls for dirty jobs – was tough and warm, and was kept clean by the ship's laundry.

▷ The rig worn for dirty jobs like painting ship or swabbing decks. These necessary jobs were fairly shared out as part of the normal daily ship's routine. Spells of extra duty on such work were ordered as practical punishments for mild offences.

◁ A carrier sailor in basic uniform, joining ship. His kitbag holds his Number 1 (best) uniform, spare underwear, shaving kit and personal effects. All other items that he needed, such as steel helmet and protective clothing, were issued by ship's supplies.

Medical facilities on board were excellent, and the sick bay of every big ship included a fully equipped operating room.

The greatest importance was attached to feeding the men. Menus were kept as varied as possible, with extensive use of frozen rather than canned food. The US Navy was the first to adopt the self-service technique, familiar today, for feeding sailors at sea. Instead of the traditional method of small groups or "messes" of sailors eating together, each man collected his own meal on a tray from a central food counter and took it to a table to eat. There were abundant supplies of iced water and soft drinks. Other comforts included showings of the latest movies from Hollywood.

These benefits were envied, even mocked, by other navies such as the British. But there was a serious purpose to their provision: the removal of as much strain as possible from the life of the sailor – to keep him healthy and efficient during prolonged service at sea.

△ "Chow time": a well-earned meal for tired crewmen of the carrier *Yorktown* in October 1943. Each man has collected his own meal on a single tray from a central food counter.

▷ Anti-aircraft gunner at his battle station, dressed in steel helmet and life-jacket.

▷ This recruiting poster for the United States Navy shows a selection of the rank badges (top) and specialist trade badges worn by enlisted (non-officer) crewmen of the American fleet.

Keeping 'em flying

Apart from submarines, the carriers' most dangerous enemies were dive-bombers and torpedo-bombers. Every man on board knew that a carrier's main defense against air attack was its own aircraft, catching and shooting down enemy aircraft before they could strike home. But some aircraft always got through, and, when they did, the carrier's last line of defense lay in its batteries of AA (anti-aircraft) guns.

Anti-aircraft gunners fought unprotected, in open gun positions, feeding clips of 20 mm and 40 mm shells into rapid-firing guns. It took supreme courage to stand and face the screaming attack of an enemy aircraft which, if not shot down, would cause the death of perhaps hundreds of the gunners' shipmates.

△ Scanning the skies: anti-aircraft gunners and loaders at their battle stations, manning one of the carrier's quadruple 40 mm gun mounts.

▷ Yeoman signallers: their mastery of the code-books and ability to flash fast, clear signals from ship to ship or from ship to air was vital.

◁ After a bomb attack a flight deck repair crew swings into action, cutting out and replacing damaged timbers and deck frames to restore the deck for flying operations.

If the carrier did suffer bomb or torpedo damage, responsibility for the defense of the ship shifted to the fire-fighting and repair crews. The first priority was always repairs to the flight deck, without which the carrier could neither recover aircraft nor launch others for the purposes of attack or defense.

△ In safe waters and fair weather, a Douglas SBD dive-bomber receives an engine service up on the flight deck.

▷ A flight deck medic: their prompt action saved the lives of many badly wounded aircrew after struggling back to their carrier.

△ Draped with belts of ammunition, ordnancemen arm a fighter for its next sortie.

▽ An officer chalks his personal message on a bomb intended for a target in Japan.

Down on the hangar decks, the aircraft repair and maintenance crews did an equally important job. Whether members of a fighter, bomber or torpedo squadron, they knew their work was vital to the flyers who naturally won the lion's share of credit for victories in the air. It was the boast of any maintenance crew chief worth his salt that he and his men could "build a whole new airplane" as long as the spare parts were there – or even, when spares ran short, using parts "cannibalized" from aircraft too damaged to repair.

A sailor's life

The sailor's day was divided into working periods known as watches which, in normal routine, left half the crew resting while the other half worked. Every man had his cruising station – the part of ship where he carried out his normal duties – and his battle station, which he manned when the ship came to full alert, ready for action.

A typical working day alternated between routine cleaning and maintenance work, and constant drills. These were aimed at clipping vital seconds off the time taken to come to battle stations, with firefighting, damage repair and medical teams at the ready, and aircraft prepared for launching. Strict fire precautions were vital because of all the fuel aboard.

◁ A carrier sailor off-watch writes a letter home before grabbing some precious "sack time" (sleep). Cramped conditions below decks meant that the men had little chance of privacy. Every effort was made to ensure that life for the sailors was as free from strain as possible during prolonged operations far from base.

Below decks, life off-duty was lived in a world of constant artificial light, with temperature and humidity controlled by air conditioning. Tropical skin complaints such as the miseries of prickly heat were thus greatly reduced. Good ventilation was important not only for the comfort of the men, but also to prevent the build-up of gasoline fumes which could cause an explosion. All living spaces were protected by watertight doors. These divided the ship into watertight compartments, ensuring the greatest possible saving of life in the event of accident or sudden enemy attack.

Though washing facilities were always far better in a big ship like a carrier than in a small ship like a destroyer or frigate, the need to save every possible drop of fresh water was drilled into every man on board. When taking a shower, the strictly enforced routine was "Wet Down – Water Off – Soap Up – Water On – Rinse Down – Water Off".

The highest value was placed on the delivery of mail to the men at sea. Of all the carefully provided comforts and aids to morale on board, few were reckoned more important than the long-awaited mail call, bringing the men the latest news from their families and hometowns thousands of miles away, back in the United States.

△ Careful calculation was needed to work out how much food was required for the crew. Here a cook opens a case of canned peaches for peach pie: fourteen cases were needed to make enough pie for the air group alone.

▷ Bunks and lockers for possessions in one of the "berthing compartments" where the men slept. Here three crewmen of the *Yorktown*, which joined the American fleet in summer 1943, play a game of cards.

"Pilots, man your planes!"

Once the aircraft of the strike force had been fueled, armed, and ranged on deck, the ship's loudspeakers blared the thrilling order of "Pilots, man your planes!". The carrier heeled as it turned into the wind. The moment of launch had arrived.

As the carrier continued to steam at full speed into the wind, with its speed of 30 knots or more boosting the strength of the wind coming down the flight deck, the fliers carried out their final cockpit checks. The most important check was on the performance of the engine, for any engine failure at the moment of takeoff would mean an inevitable crash into the sea in front of the carrier's oncoming bow.

Out on the flight deck, where the firefighting teams and medical crews were poised to tackle any emergency, the noise was deafening when the pilots roared their engines to full throttle. As each aircraft was positioned on the centerline of the flight deck for takeoff, the pilot kept his eyes on the deck officer's hand. This was "wound up" to signal the pilot to push his engine to full power, then swept down as the order to "Go!".

The first to go was the commander of each squadron, leading his men into the air and directing them into their flying formation. Any aircraft crashing on the flight deck during takeoff – from a burst tire or undercarriage failure – had first to be rendered safe by the firefighting teams, then manhandled out of the way to clear the deck for the aircraft waiting behind.

During launch, the attention of every man on board was focused on the event. It was a moment of almost unbearable tension, for any lapse of concentration could bring about a disastrous accident. The fate of a battle could turn on the speed with which the aircraft could get into the air. And until the last aircraft had gone, the carrier could not turn out of the wind and resume its defensive zigzag course, the best protection against torpedo attack from enemy submarines.

△ The carrier's flag, or ensign, streams in the wind which blows straight down the flight deck. With the roar of the plane's engine battering the eardrums of the flight-deck crews, a Hellcat fighter pilot watches the hand signals of the deck officer controlling the launch.

15

Strike force airborne

The last great carrier-versus-carrier battle of the Pacific war was the Battle of the Philippine Sea (June 19–20, 1944). It was fought between the Japanese First Mobile Fleet, with a total of nine carriers of all sizes, and the American Fifth Fleet of fifteen carriers.

The Fifth Fleet was covering the American invasion of Saipan in the Marianas Islands: an invasion which the Japanese had to defeat in order to defend their home islands. Despite his enormous advantage in numbers in both carriers and aircraft (the Fifth Fleet numbered 900 aircraft of all types), the American Admiral, Raymond A. Spruance, chose to let the Japanese open the battle and make the first attacks.

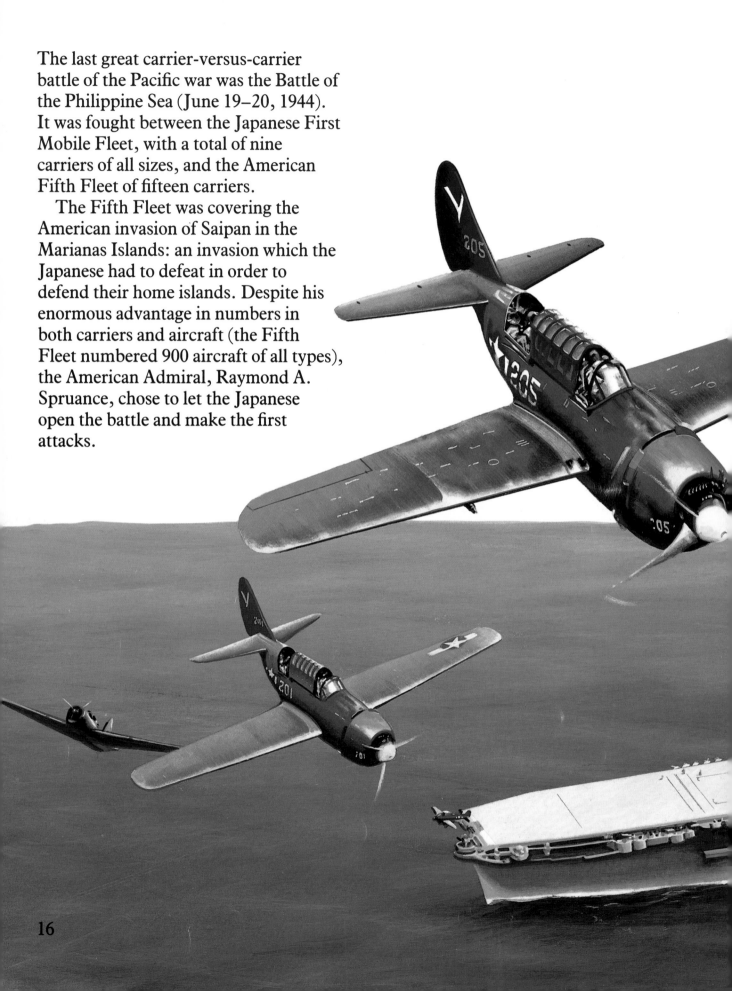

The battle was won in the air on June 19 by the massed Hellcat fighters of the Fifth Fleet. On that day they shot down so many Japanese carrier aircraft that the Americans remember the Battle of the Philippine Sea as "The Great Marianas Turkey Shoot." Of the 373 planes that took off from the Japanese carriers, only 130 got back. But when, on 20 June, the Americans launched

their main attack of 77 dive-bombers, 54 torpedo-bombers and 85 escorting fighters, only 14 American aircraft were lost. By nightfall on June 20, with only 35 carrier aircraft left, the Japanese fleet had no choice but to retreat. It was a crushing defeat for the Japanese carrier force, for it was impossible to replace the loss of so many aircraft and trained aircrew.

The Americans won the Battle of the Philippine Sea because of the huge numbers of fighter planes which their carriers were able to put into the air. At one stage they even sent off their Helldiver dive-bombers to circle overhead, in order to leave the flight decks clear for more fighters to be launched and recovered.

◁ On the first day of the Battle of the Philippine Sea, Helldiver dive-bombers circle over an American Essex-class carrier as the American Fifth Fleet throws up its huge shield of fighters to break the Japanese attacks.

Enemy attack!

At the beginning of World War II,
before any experience had been gained
of what air attacks by fast-moving
aircraft were really like, aircraft carriers
had nothing like the anti-aircraft gun
defenses they were carrying by 1945.
There was too much reliance on heavy
guns, designed to throw up a high anti-
aircraft protective "umbrella" over
the ship.

To stop a dive-bomber, plunging from 6,000 m (20,000 ft), heavy AA guns were not enough. The first carrier battles of the Coral Sea and Midway, in May and June 1942, showed what was really needed. This was a massed array of lighter, rapid-firing guns which could keep enemy planes under constant fire, no matter from what angle they came.

The carrier *Yorktown*, sunk at Midway, was armed with eight single 5-inch AA guns. But the giant *Midway*, built in 1944–5 (though it did not see action), had eighteen 5-inch guns and 84 rapid firing 40 mm guns, mounted in 21 groups of four.

These AA gunners worked in two-man teams. The gunner had to keep his guns on target, swinging them up and down and from side to side, while firing. The loader's job was to feed in the clips of shells, keeping them coming in a steady stream. A loader who got his rhythm wrong and let his guns fall silent at the crucial moment could give an enemy pilot enough time to drop his bomb on target.

The gun mountings were positioned to cover all possible angles of approach by enemy aircraft. There was an obvious danger that one gun crew, swinging its guns to keep the target in its sights, might accidentally fire into the ship itself. This danger was overcome by fitting each gun mounting with a "limit stop."

Few men in the ship – apart from the fliers of the air group – were more exposed to enemy fire than the AA gunners. They were the last line of defense, both for their ship and their shipmates.

◁ As a blazing Japanese plane plunges towards the carrier, a battery of 40 mm guns desperately tries to blow it up in the air before it can crash into the ship and explode. On the far side of the carrier, the portside guns, mounted beneath the edge of the flight deck, continue to fire at other aircraft. Below the 40 mm battery in the foreground can be seen the turrets of the aft 5-inch guns, with their twin barrels fully elevated to send up the next high-level anti-aircraft barrage.

Damage control

Without armor plate to protect the supplies of aviation fuel, oil, bombs, torpedoes and shells, fire was always one of the carrier's deadliest enemies. The importance of the firefighting and damage-control crews in saving the ship from disaster was proved by the experiences of two American carriers early in the Pacific war.

On May 8, 1942, in the Battle of the Coral Sea, the *Lexington* was hit by two small bombs and two torpedoes. The bombs started fires in an ammunition box and the smokestack structure, but these were quickly put out. The most serious damage was caused by the two torpedo hits, but this, too, was brought under control. *Lexington* was restored to an even keel by pumping fuel oil from one side of the ship to the other, and all planes still in the air were recovered. But the Japanese attacks had released deadly gasoline fumes from cracked tanks and fuel lines that eventually blew up in a shattering series of explosions deep in the ship. Massive internal fires could not be controlled by the firefighting crews, and the ship had to be abandoned.

At Midway (June 4, 1942) the *Yorktown* was hit by three bombs in her first Japanese attack. These started separate fires on the hangar deck, in the rag storage space (with shells and fuel stored close by), and three decks down, knocking out the engines. All three fires were put out and the *Yorktown* re-entered the battle, only to be hit by two torpedoes in a second attack. These fires, too, were put out, but the destruction of the forward generator room left her without electric power to carry out vital repairs.

The ship was still afloat two days later, with a destroyer alongside providing power for repair work, when her other side was ripped open by two torpedoes from a Japanese submarine. This last attack undid all the superb work done by the *Yorktown*'s firefighters and damage-control crews and sank the carrier, but priceless lessons had been learned which were put to good use in later battles.

▷ After a savage air attack by the Japanese in November 1944, firefighters of the carrier *Intrepid* swarm in to extinguish dozens of small fires burning fiercely on the wooden flight deck. Fires like these were often widely scattered by debris flying from explosions, and had to be smothered at once – often under enemy attack – before they could take hold and spread.

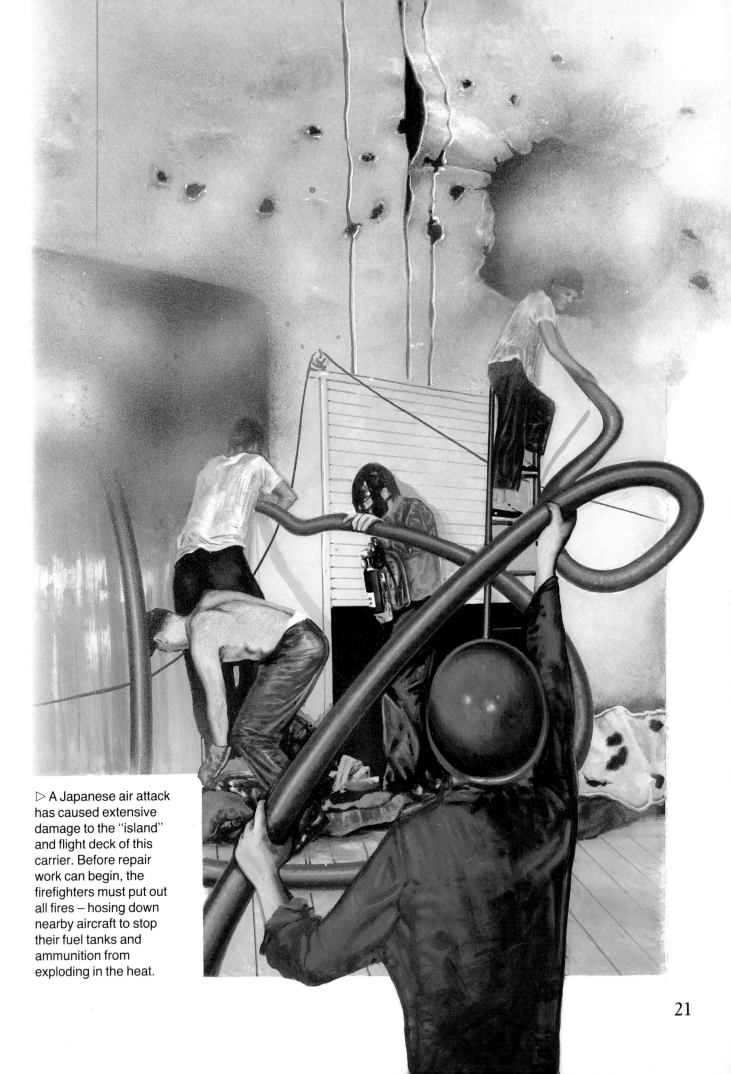

▷ A Japanese air attack has caused extensive damage to the "island" and flight deck of this carrier. Before repair work can begin, the firefighters must put out all fires – hosing down nearby aircraft to stop their fuel tanks and ammunition from exploding in the heat.

Recovering aircraft

Recovering aircraft after an attack was always a moment of high tension aboard a carrier. As at takeoff, the ship had to steam steadily into the wind rather than following a protective, zigzag course. This made her an easier target for any enemy submarine in the area. During aircraft recovery, a carrier was also very vulnerable to enemy air attack. There were many occasions when returning aircraft had to be told to stay clear, as the carrier prepared to beat off attacking aircraft.

But the real cause of concern was the condition of the returning aircraft and their crews. The planes were likely to be running short of fuel, and many would have suffered battle damage and be carrying wounded or badly injured crew on board.

Battle damage took many forms, and if a plane's radio had been destroyed the pilot could not radio ahead to warn the carrier of his plight. Every approaching aircraft was therefore anxiously watched for signs of damage or distress. The flight-deck recovery crews – firefighters, stretcher bearers, and aircraft handlers – had to be ready for anything.

An aircraft trailing smoke spelled an obvious fire risk, while many flight-deck crashes were caused by damaged undercarriages. After such crashes, the aircrew had to be extricated and the wreck moved aside to permit the next aircraft to land. Speed was vital, for many of the returning planes desperately needed to touch down before their last reserves of fuel ran out.

An aircraft whose undercarriage failed on landing could easily cartwheel off its line of approach, smashing into other aircraft or even into the sea. Many lives were saved by the device known as the crash barrier: a flexible net raised above the deck. The crash barrier halted helplessly skidding aircraft, enabling rescue, medical aid and deck clearance work to begin at once.

◁ The scene aboard a carrier during aircraft recovery. A rescue team is about to dash to help the crew of a plane which has suffered undercarriage failure on touching down, skidding along the deck before coming to a halt. Once the crew have been helped to safety, the aircraft will be cleared from the flight deck and carried down on the elevator to the waiting maintenance crews on the hangar deck. Overhead, three more planes circle awaiting their turn to land.

Relaxation on board

By the last year of the war, American carrier fleets or "task forces," supplied and refueled at sea, were spending up to three months on successive operations before returning to base. When Admiral William F. Halsey led the Third Fleet back to its base at Ulithi Atoll on January 25, 1945, its carriers had been at sea for the past 84 days.

This did not mean, of course, that the Third Fleet had been continually *in action*

for 84 days. Nor does it mean that its crew had never had a day's rest before returning to Ulithi for prolonged "R and R" (Rest and Recreation). There had been many days of peaceful steaming from one objective to the next, when the men off watch could indulge in a wide range of leisure activities on board.

An aircraft carrier was ideally suited for such purposes. When not in use for flying operations, the flight deck offered a

▽ In the well of the lowered elevator, off-watch crew members play basketball, while an audience watches from above.

spacious sports field in good weather, and sporting activities were encouraged as a way of keeping fit.

An ever-popular game was basketball, in which the obvious danger of losing the ball over the side was avoided by using the elevator well. With the elevator lowered, the well made an ideal basketball court or boxing ring, with plenty of space for spectators, who enjoyed a splendid view from above.

Runners could clock up the miles by completing lap after lap of the flight deck, while for the less athletically minded sunbathing was a popular pastime.

Movie fans were also well catered for aboard carriers, and the arrival of the latest movies from home was awaited almost as anxiously as the mail. A cleared section of the hangar deck could hold a sizable audience for films and other entertainments. The "silver screen" and the far-off world of Hollywood, avidly followed in movie magazines, was a natural antidote to the confines of the ship and the perils of war.

▽ Night scene on the hangar deck of the *Yorktown*. In the foreground ordnancemen on watch service bombs amid F6F "Hellcat" fighters. In the background men off watch take in the latest movie.

Kamikaze!

In the last year of the Pacific war, the American fleet came under increasing attack from the most dangerous tactic used by the Japanese in the entire war.

This was the suicide or kamikaze attack: an attempt to knock out or sink one warship for every aircraft sacrificed. The kamikaze pilot volunteered to become a human bomb, deliberately crashing his aircraft (usually carrying one or more bombs for greater destructive effect) into an Allied warship. From the start of the kamikaze attacks in October 1944, aircraft carriers were always the favorite targets.

The whole idea was frightening and incredible to Americans, and to their British allies. On both sides there had been many cases of dying pilots deliberately crashing into enemy ships in their last seconds of life, but this was different. Kamikaze pilots had vowed to serve their country by dying, causing as much damage as they could in their last dive. By the spring of 1945, as the Americans and British approached the Japanese home islands, the Japanese had more kamikaze volunteers than there were aircraft for them to fly.

The kamikaze attacks reached their height during the Battle of Okinawa (April–July 1945) when a total of 1,809 suicide planes were hurled at the American Fifth Fleet. Though 930 of these were shot down, by June 22, when the last mass attacks ceased, seventeen warships had been sunk and 198 damaged, including no fewer than twelve aircraft carriers and ten battleships.

The worst American casualty was the carrier *Franklin*. The bombs carried by her attacker exploded among the fueled and armed aircraft in the hangar, killing 832 men and wounding 270.

▽ As one kamikaze explodes on the flight deck, another comes roaring in from the port bow.

▷ Grim aftermath of a kamikaze attack, as a carrier crew buries its dead with full military honors.

Victory in Tokyo Bay

The war ended when Japan surrendered on August 15, 1945. Admiral Halsey warned the men of the Third Fleet to stay on their guard, because there was still a chance of desperate kamikazes disobeying the surrender order and attacking. Halsey ordered that after the surrender, "any ex-enemy aircraft attacking the fleet is to be shot down in friendly fashion."

So ended the greatest sea war in the history of the world. It had been won with amazing speed, largely because of the work of the aircraft carriers. When Japan had attacked Pearl Harbor on December 7, 1941, the American Navy had still relied on battleships, but by 1945 the carriers had become the most important heavy ships in naval warfare. Only three of America's seven carriers were in the Pacific when the war began, though six of them eventually served there and four were sunk (the *Lexington*, *Yorktown*, *Wasp*, and *Hornet*).

When Japan surrendered, the American carrier fleet had grown to the huge total of sixteen carriers, operating 1,191 aircraft between them, helped by the four carriers of the British Pacific Fleet with their 225 aircraft. The aircraft of the Third Fleet flew their last joint mission on August 22, 1945: a massed victory flyby of 1,100 aircraft over the Third Fleet lying in Tokyo Bay, known as "Operation Tintype." For the thousands of carrier sailors watching below it was a proud and thrilling moment.

But the carriers' work did not end with

▷ The date is August 22, 1945. A week has passed since Japan's surrender. As the Third Fleet lies in Tokyo Bay, the roar of a thousand engines fills the air as, in "Operation Tintype," the massed carrier aircraft of the fleet carry out the victory flight hailing the end of the Pacific war.

▽ The "Tintype" flypast photographed from a British battleship with the US Third Fleet.

28

the coming of peace in the Pacific. Japan's surrender was the signal for the release of thousands of prisoners of war, many of whom had been captives of the Japanese for over three years. Many were in urgent need of medical attention, and all were eager to return home as soon as possible. With their extensive hangar decks cleared of planes and filled with rows of cots, the carriers proved ideal transport ships for speeding the return of the former prisoners eastward across the Pacific to their homes in the United States.

Glossary

AVGAS Aviation fuel.

Battery An array of guns of the same caliber.

Battle stations State of ship's readiness with every man posted for maximum fighting capacity.

Bow The forward end of a ship.

Bridge Ship's command center, usually sited high in the superstructure.

Class Ships of the same type, named after the first such ship completed (for example, Essex-class carriers).

Clip A batch of shells for quick-firing guns, clipped together for rapid loading.

Cockpit Area containing the seat, controls and instruments of an aircraft.

Cruising stations Normal state of ship's readiness, when there is no danger of enemy action.

Destroyer Light, fast warship armed with guns and torpedoes, used mainly in escorting and scouting for fleets.

Dive-bomber Attack aircraft designed to drop its bombs in a steep dive.

Fighter Aircraft designed to shoot down other aircraft; may also carry bombs (fighter-bomber).

Flight deck The flat upper deck of a carrier, used for launching and recovering aircraft.

▷ Major carrier battles in the Pacific, 1942–5.
1 Coral Sea, May 1942
2 Midway, June 1942
3 Eastern Solomons, August – 1942
4 Santa Cruz, October 1942
5 Philippine Sea, June 1944
6 Leyte Gulf, October 1944

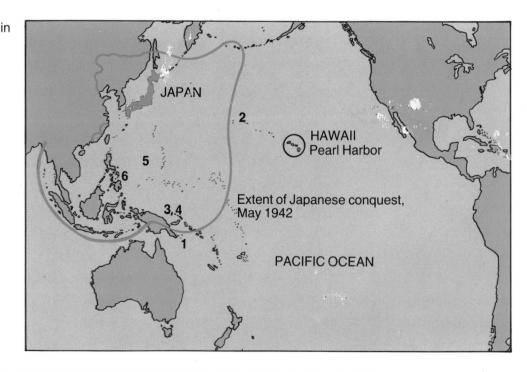

Timechart

Hangar deck Located below a carrier's flight deck; used for accommodating and servicing aircraft.

Island The carrier's superstructure, containing the bridge on the starboard or right-hand side of the flight deck.

Knot A speed of a nautical mile an hour. A nautical mile is 1,852 m (6,080 ft).

Ordnanceman Crewman who services weapons and replenishes aircraft with ammunition, bombs and torpedoes.

Portside The left-hand side of a ship, facing forward.

Squadron Unit of airmen, identified by number (for example, Fighting 1, Bombing 6, Torpedo 3, etc.).

Starboard The right-hand side of a ship facing forward.

Stern The rear end of a ship.

Torpedo Fast-running, self-propelled missile designed to explode against a ship's side under water.

Torpedo-bomber Aircraft designed to drop either bombs or a torpedo.

Watch A period of duty for a member of the ship's crew, who would rest when off watch.

December 7, 1941 Japanese carrier attack on Pearl Harbor opens the Pacific war.

May 8, 1942 Battle of the Coral Sea, first carrier-versus-carrier battle in history, halts tide of Japanese conquest.

June 4, 1942 Battle of Midway; four Japanese carriers sunk.

August 1942–February 1943 Battle of Guadalcanal begins American reconquest of the Pacific.

February 1944 American carriers attack Japanese base at Truk in Central Pacific.

June 19–20, 1944 Battle of the Philippine Sea, last great carrier-versus-carrier battle. Three Japanese carriers sunk and 92 percent of Japanese carrier planes destroyed.

October 20–25, 1944 Americans land in Philippines; three Japanese battleships, four Japanese carriers sunk. End of opposition by Japanese Navy.

February 19, 1945 Americans land on Iwo Jima.

April–May 1945 During battle for Okinawa, American carrier fleet endures mass kamikaze attacks.

July 1945 US Third Fleet begins attack on Japan.

August 6, 1945 First atomic bomb dropped on Hiroshima.

August 15, 1945 End of hostilities.

September 2, 1945 Japanese surrender signed in Tokyo Bay.

Index

PRINTED IN BELGIUM BY

INTERNATIONAL BOOK PRODUCTION